THE ELEPHANT REPAIRMAN

Funny Poems for Kids

Kenn Nesbitt

Illustrations by
Rafael Domingos

Copyright © 2022 by Kenn Nesbitt

Internal design © 2022 by Purple Room Publishing

Cover design by Rafael Domingos

All rights reserved. No part of this book may be reproduced in any form or by any electronic or mechanical means, including information storage and retrieval systems—except in the case of brief quotations embodied in critical articles or reviews—without permission in writing from its publisher, Purple Room Publishing.

Published by
Purple Room Publishing
1037 NE 65th St #81845
Seattle, WA 98115

Fax: 800-991-2996
ATTN: Purple Room Publishing #81845

www.poetry4kids.com

For Leslie and John

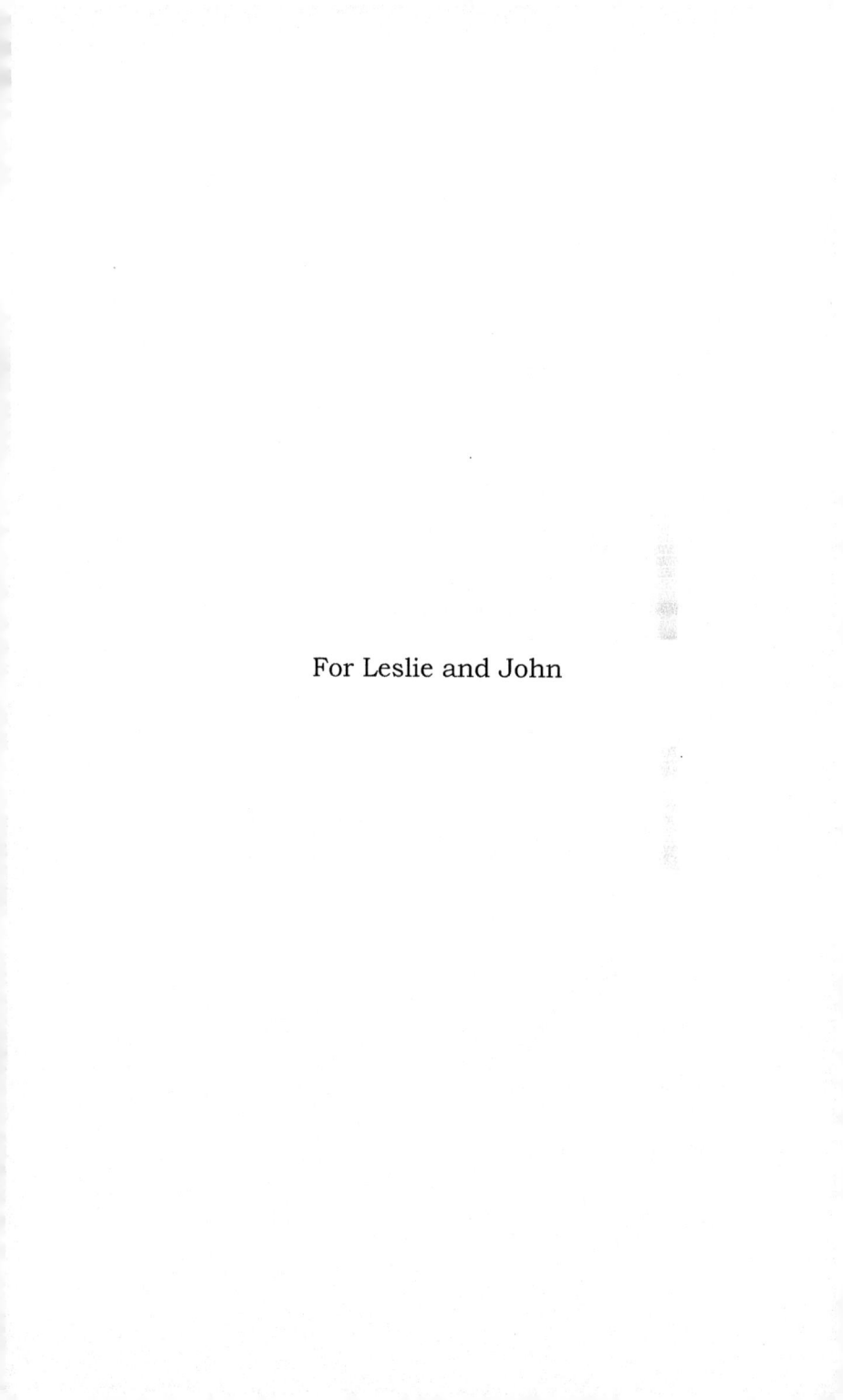

Contents

The Elephant Repairman 8

Computer Cat 10

Our Magic Toilet 12

Astrocow 14

The Noisy Boys from Boise 16

Crash! Bang! Boom! 18

Our Classroom Is Covered in Sparkles 20

I Tried to Find a Dinosaur 21

I Hypnotized the Teacher 22

Elaine the Complainer 24

I Think I'd Like to Get a Pet 26

My Sloth Is Supersonic 28

Tiny Todd the Turtle 30

A Rumble in My Bedroom 32

I Like It When It's Quiet 33

Mr. Whisper 34

I Love to Read a Mystery 36

The Book of Glue	38
Today I Have a Toothache	39
Toucan Can-Can	40
I'm Wearing My Parrot	41
My Koala's Not a Doctor	42
My Kitten Had an Accident	44
The Weather Is Perfect for Running	45
Overslept	46
Zoom Gloom	48
Please Don't Prank Your Parents	50
The Life of a Pirate Ain't Easy	52
My Brother Was Brought by a Bunny	54
How to Eat a Chocolate Bunny	56
My Sister Should Be an Explorer	58
Somewhere, Sometime	59
I Went to the Movies	60
Pickle with Cheddar	62
The Geese Are Honking Overhead	64
Our Baseball Team Is Always Last	65

I Went to a Wishing Well 66

My Grandma Bought a Rocking Chair 68

The Cow on the Hill 70

My Ice Cream Is Melting 71

My Hot Dog Is Soggy 72

Candy Andy 74

Mrs. Mandy's Candy Shop 76

Random Recipe 78

If You're Swallowed by an Elephant 79

I Went Out Exploring 80

Transportation Vacation 82

The First Day of School 83

The Birds Are Chirping Happily 84

I've Started Learning Honkish 86

Octopus for Lunch 88

My Brother Plays Dungeons and Dragons 91

Mr. Right 92

My Left Left 94

My World Is Turning Downside-Up 96

I'm Srot of Srcmabled Up Tdaoy 98

Saturday's My Lazy Day 99

I'd Like to Sing in Singapore 100

I Got a New Game for My Brother 102

My Parents Both Are Humans 103

We Bought a Lot of Candy Bars 104

It's Halloween, My Face Is Green 106

A Vampire Bit My Neck Last Night 108

My Brother Might Be Bigfoot 110

I'd Like to Meet an Alien 112

The Dog Ate Our Dinner 114

I Dreamed It Was December 116

Our Holiday Shopping 118

Hip-Hop Christmas 120

On New Year's Day 122

The Elephant Repairman

If your elephant is broken
and she needs a quick repair,
call the elephant repairman
and he'll instantly be there.

If her trunk can't play the trumpet
or her toes can't tap a beat,
then the elephant repairman will
inspect her nose and feet.

If her tail won't hold a kite string,
if her ears won't make her fly,
then the elephant repairman
will explain the reason why.

When he figures out the problem
then he'll start on the repair
with his elephant repair kit,
which he carries everywhere.

And it's guaranteed your elephant
will soon be good as new
since repairing broken elephants
is what he likes to do.

But he cannot fix your dinosaur,
your dragon, or your duck.
So, if one of them is broken,
I'm afraid you're out of luck.

Computer Cat

Some cats like growling,
and some like to purr,
and others like napping
or licking their fur.
But my cat is different
and she would prefer
to use the computer all day.

She's somewhat surprising,
not like other cats.
She blogs about dogs
and she reads about rats.
She loves online shopping
and video chats,
and searching for games she can play.

As long as the Internet's
working just fine,
my cat's on my laptop
and surfing online.
She likes it so much that
this kitty of mine
will never go out of the house.

She learned how to code
to control the machine
by clicking the keyboard
and swiping the screen.
But, why does she do it?
From what I have seen,
it's mostly to play with the mouse.

Our Magic Toilet

We have a magic toilet.
It makes things disappear.
Just toss them in and flip the switch
and—Presto!—they're not here.

We love our magic toilet.
It's super fun to use.
My brother flushed his baseball bat.
My sister flushed her shoes.

The baby flushed her bottle.
I flushed my radio.
It's crazy how things vanish
but we don't know where they go.

Our mother flushed the sofa.
She flushed our camping tent.
That's when I looked around and said,
"I wonder where dad went?"

Astrocow

Hello, my name is AstroCow.
I'm deep in outer space right now.
I'm off to visit distant stars.
I've seen the moon. I've been to Mars.

I've done the most amazing things.
I soared through Saturn's massive rings.
I checked out Neptune. Pluto too.
Then out among the stars I flew.

I built this awesome rocket ship
to take an interstellar trip,
and travel through the galaxy
to find a home for cows like me.

You see, I used to live on Earth.
It was my home, my place of birth.
But now I search for somewhere new;
somewhere they don't serve barbecue.

The Noisy Boys from Boise

The Noisy Boys from Boise
are the noisiest of boys.
They're boisterous annoyances.
They're great at making noise.

They wake up every morning
with a COCK-A-DOODLE-DOO!
And then they start to BARK! and HONK!
and OINK! and CLUCK! and MOO!

At breakfast time they throw their bowls
to hear the way they SMASH!
They fill the room with BAM! and BOOM!
and BASH! and CRACK! and CRASH!

They STOMP and TROMP around the house
until it's time for lunch,
then POUND their plates with hammers
for the CLATTER and the CRUNCH!

They CLANG on cans and pots and pans,
then BANG the dinner bell,
which means it's time to SLURP! and BURP!
and run around and YELL!

And when they go to bed
they're even louder than before.
The Noisy Boys from Boise sleep…
and SNORE, and SNORE, and SNORE!

Crash! Bang! Boom!

I close my eyes, turn off the light.
CRASH! BANG! BOOM!

Oh, what's that noise so late at night?
CRASH! BANG! BOOM!

It seems that something isn't right.
CRASH! BANG! BOOM!

It's giving me an awful fright.
CRASH! BANG! BOOM!

Is it some fiend I'll have to fight?
CRASH! BANG! BOOM!

Or could it be a bat in flight?
CRASH! BANG! BOOM!

I shine my flashlight, nice and bright.
CRASH! BANG! BOOM!

My brother's playing drums tonight!
CRASH! BANG! BOOM!

Our Classroom Is Covered in Sparkles

Our classroom is covered in sparkles
and tinsel that twinkles and shines.
The kids are all caked with confetti that glows
with glistening rainbow designs.

Our teacher is spattered with spangles.
She's shimmering, shiny, and bright.
She looks like a disco ball burst overhead
and splashed her with speckles of light.

Our desks are all glimmering brightly.
The chairs and the carpets are gleaming.
There isn't a surface inside of our room
that isn't bedazzling and beaming.

Our janitor's grumpy and grumbling.
To him it's just that much more litter.
But, still, we love sharing our Valentine's cards
in envelopes loaded with glitter.

I Tried to Find a Dinosaur

I tried to find a dinosaur.
I started in my yard.
I dug and dug for days and days.
The work was long and hard.

I dug through dirt and mud and muck.
I dug through rocks and soil.
My arms grew sore. My legs grew weak
from all the sweat and toil.

I shoveled tons of gravel out.
I moved a bunch of stones,
until, at last, to my surprise,
I found some fossil bones.

I put the bones together in
my bedroom on the floor.
When I was done, those bones had formed
a half a dinosaur.

My parents weren't too happy when
I told them of my goal.
I found a half a dinosaur,
but then they found the hole.

I Hypnotized the Teacher

I hypnotized the teacher
in our classroom yesterday.
I think it worked! He's started
doing everything I say.

I said he was a chicken.
He began to crow and cluck.
And then he started quacking
when I said he was a duck.

It made my classmates laugh
to see the teacher act so funny.
He hopped and nibbled carrots
when I said he was a bunny.

I said he was a fierce,
ferocious, giant dinosaur.
It worked, but now he won't do
what I tell him anymore.

Our class is now directed by
this stomping, roaring creature.
I recommend that you don't ever
hypnotize your teacher.

Elaine the Complainer

My name is Elaine
and I like to complain.
Complaining is all that I do.
I moan when it's hot
and I groan when it's not.
I whine when the sky is too blue.

I fuss that the food
on my plate must be chewed.
I whimper whenever I clean.
I frequently fret
if my bath gets me wet.
I gripe if the grass is too green.

I act like my brain
is in terrible pain
when people are being polite.
But then, if they're rude,
it will ruin my mood;
I'll grumble and mumble all night.

But though I delight
in complaining all night,
there's one thing I simply can't see.
I don't understand
(since I'm clearly so grand)
why people complain about me.

I Think I'd Like to Get a Pet

I think I'd like to get a pet.
I don't know which one I should get.
Should it be big? Should it be small?
Should it be short or super tall?

Should it be bald or very hairy?
Should it be cute or sort of scary?
Should it be friendly, mean, or shy?
And should it swim, or should it fly?

Should it have feathers, fins, or fur?
Should it prefer to bark or purr?
Should it be one that squeaks or squawks,
or maybe one that goes for walks?

Should it be one with stripes, or spots,
or green and purple polka dots?
Should it be brown, or blue, or pink?
I wonder what my mom would think.

I wonder if she'd even let
me go and get myself a pet.
And, so, I hope she doesn't mind
when I get one of every kind.

My Sloth Is Supersonic

My sloth is supersonic
as she sprints around my room.
She flies so fast you'll often hear her
cause a sonic boom.

My snail is also speedy.
He's the fastest snail alive.
I've seen him flash right past me
when I'm going for a drive.

My turtle hurtles faster than
the record-breaking pace.
So, naturally, my sloth and snail
and turtle love to race.

A week ago, my pets were slow,
which leads me to conclude
they got this way the day
I started feeding them fast food.

Tiny Todd the Turtle

My turtle's name is Tiny Todd.
He's Tiny Todd the turtle.
And Tiny Todd the turtle's favorite
game to play is Wordle.

He has to guess a random word
by typing on his phone.
He's never lost a single game.
His record stands alone.

He starts it every morning
and he plays till late at night.
It always takes him all day long
to get the answer right.

He tries to play it fast, and yet
his pace is just a crawl,
since Tiny Todd the turtle's
still a turtle after all.

A Rumble in My Bedroom

There's a rumble in my bedroom
like I've never felt before.
I can see it on the ceiling.
I can feel it on the floor.

All my furniture is juddering
and jumping 'round the room,
and the sound is loud and pounding
like a constant sonic boom.

There's a banging and a clanging
and a thudding and a thumping.
I can barely even stand
with all the shaking and the bumping.

And it's been this way since yesterday.
It hasn't let up yet.
Man, I never knew a kangaroo
was such a crummy pet.

I Like It When It's Quiet

I like it when it's quiet;
when no one says a word.
I'm happy when there's not
a single sound that can be heard.

I love it when it's silent
and peaceful as a dream.
Whenever it gets noisy,
it makes me want to scream.

It makes me want to holler.
It makes me want to shout.
It makes me want to screech and shriek
and huff and puff and pout.

It makes me want to rant and rave.
It makes me want to roar.
It makes me want to yowl and howl
and hammer on the floor.

And so I throw a tantrum
and I yell and run around
until it's peaceful as a dream
and no one makes a sound.

Mr. Whisper

Mr. Whisper's quiet.
He's a silent sort of guy.
He whispers everything he says,
though no one quite knows why.

He murmurs, speaking softly,
and his words sound like a sigh.
His voice is barely louder than
a flapping butterfly.

You'll have to pay attention
if you want to hear him speak.
And, yet, you may not understand;
his voice is rather weak.

It's best to walk right up to him,
and lean in nice and near,
then turn your head and use one hand,
or both, to cup your ear.

But if you still can't figure out
the tale he's trying to tell,
go get a quick translation
from his buddy, Mr. Yell.

I Love to Read a Mystery

I love to read a mystery.
It's my favorite kind of book.
There's one I like a lot about
a butler and a cook.
I had it here this morning.
It was in my reading nook.
But now my book is missing.
Was it stolen by a crook?
I wonder if my mystery was
the only thing they took.

I hope that I can find it.
Will you come and help me look?
Then we can solve "The Mystery
of the Missing Mystery Book."

The Book of Glue

I wrote a book, *The Book of Glue*,
a little while ago.
I'd love to let you read it but
I just can't let it go.

If I could let you borrow it,
I promise I would do it,
except I can't. See, that's my story
and I'm sticking to it.

Today I Have a Toothache

Today I have a toothache.
I feel like I could cry.
I don't know how it happened.
I cannot tell you why.

I look down at my wristwatch
and wonder if I'm mental.
My watch says it's tooth-hurty.
Is that coinci-*dental*?

Toucan Can-Can

If a toucan has a tutu
she can do the can-can dance.
(The can-can is a dance that
tutu'd toucans do in France.)

When a toucan does the tutu can-can,
two can can-can too.
So, if you have a tutu too
to can-can, so can you.

I'm Wearing My Parrot

I'm wearing my parrot. He's here on my hair.
My snake's in the sleeve of my shirt.
My lizard is lounging around on my pack.
My frog is attached to my skirt.

My grasshopper's hopping on top of my socks.
My turtle is perched on my toes.
I dressed up this way since it's St. Patrick's Day,
and I don't have any green clothes.

My Koala's Not a Doctor

My koala's not a doctor.
My koala's not a teacher.
My koala's not a pilot.
My koala's not a preacher.

My koala's not an actor,
or an athlete, or musician.
My koala's not a writer,
or a lawyer, or magician.

My koala's not a scientist.
He's not a film director.
My koala's not an astronaut.
He's not a trash collector.

My koala's pretty lazy.
He just hangs out in a tree,
and he never went to school
for a diploma or degree.

So he couldn't get a job
at any place where he applied.
My koala's unemployed because
he's unkoalafied.

My Kitten Had an Accident

My kitten had an accident.
She whimpered, wept, and wailed.
She played near an electric fan
and got herself detailed.

But now she's good as new
and feeling better than before.
She bought herself a brand-new tail
down at the retail store.

The Weather Is Perfect for Running

The weather is perfect for running.
I think that I'll go for a jog.
Except I'm a little bit tired,
so maybe I'll just walk the dog.

But he seems too hyper for walking.
He looks kind of hard to control.
So maybe I'll leave him at home,
and go for a leisurely stroll.

But all of my socks are too dirty,
and all of my shoes are untied.
So maybe I'll sit on the front porch.
Or maybe I'll just stay inside.

I see that my kitten is purring,
and wants to curl up on my lap.
It wouldn't be right to prevent her
from getting her afternoon nap.

It's comfortable here on the sofa.
My pillows are cozy and deep.
The weather is perfect for running.
So that's why I'm going to sleep.

Overslept

I overslept. I woke up late.
I had to rush. I couldn't wait.
I grabbed my clothes. I threw them on.
And, in an instant, I was gone.
I ran to school. When I got there,
my friends and classmates stopped to stare.

I looked a mess, without a doubt.
I had my coat on inside out.
It seems I wore my sister's shirt.
My trouser legs were caked with dirt.
One shoe was green. The other, red,
and underwear was on my head.

I thought that everyone would frown
and call me names and put me down.
But then, instead of what I feared,
my friends applauded, whooped, and cheered.
It turns out people think it's cool
when you're the worst-dressed kid in school.

Zoom Gloom

Distance learning. What a bore.
Our school's been closed a month or more.
I'm stuck at home. I'm in my room,
and meeting with my class on Zoom.

There's no more lunchroom. No PE.
Just studying and tests for me.
There's no more recess. No more ball.
Just staring at my bedroom wall.

The playground's closed—the swings, the slide—
and everybody's stuck inside.
We can't go out and play with friends.
I hope that, pretty soon, this ends.

I know it's only for a while,
but here's a thought that makes me smile:
Although it might not sound so cool,
I just can't *wait* to go to school.

Please Don't Prank Your Parents

When April Fool's Day comes this year
please follow this advice:
You *shouldn't* prank your parents.
Nope. That isn't very nice.

To make it easy, here's a list
of things you shouldn't do:
The bathroom floor is not the place
to put your plastic poo.

Don't turn the family photos
upside down around the house.
And never tape the underside
of mom's computer mouse.

Don't change the menus on the TV
into Gunganese.
Don't offer dad a sandwich
with the plastic on the cheese.

Don't place a piece of tinfoil
in their bed beneath the sheet.
Don't stick some ketchup packets
underneath the toilet seat.

You really shouldn't use the salt
to fill the sugar bowl.
Of course, leave all the batteries
in each remote control.

Don't set the clocks an hour ahead
to make them think they're late.
And bubble wrap beneath the bathmat
might make them irate.

So, that's a list of April Fool's Day
pranks you shouldn't do.
(Unless you need to get them back
for pranks they played on you.)

The Life of a Pirate Ain't Easy

The life of a pirate ain't easy.
You'll have to buy lots of supplies.
A parrot for one of your shoulders.
An eyepatch for one of your eyes.

Before you set sail for adventure,
before you embark on your trip,
you'll need to come up with the money
to purchase a suitable ship.

You'll need a new chest for your treasure,
a hat and a flag and a plank,
some boots and a spyglass and compass,
which might take a loan from the bank.

Along with this other equipment,
you'll need a new hook and a peg,
and these are the priciest items;
they'll cost you an arm and a leg.

My Brother Was Brought by a Bunny

My brother was brought by a bunny.
He came in a basket today
surrounded by candy and chocolates.
I'm shocked that he showed up this way.

And, somehow, he's tinted with zigzags
and covered with colorful dots.
He's stippled with sparkles and spangles.
He's slathered with splashes and spots.

My brother's as bright as a rainbow.
He's yellow and purple and red.
And, strangely, I don't see his stomach.
And, also, I can't find his head.

I can't find his back or his bottom.
I don't see an arm or a leg.
It's weird but, because I'm a chicken,
my brother arrived as an egg.

How to Eat a Chocolate Bunny

First, you take the chocolate bunny
and you nibble on his nose.
Then you bite his back and belly
and you taste his tail and toes.

Then you shovel down his shoulders
and you ruminate his rear.
Then you feast upon his face
before you eat an eye and ear.

Then you giggle like a goofball
just because it's all so funny.
Then you tell your sister, "Sorry,"
since you ate her chocolate bunny.

My Sister Should Be an Explorer

My sister should be an explorer
and travel the world far and near.
I think she should see every country.
I think it could take a whole year.

She'd probably climb many mountains.
She'd sail all the oceans and seas.
She might even learn a new language,
like Spanish, or French, or Chinese.

She'd see all the wonders of nature,
like glaciers, volcanoes, and caves.
She'd find the best rivers for rafting,
and beaches for surfing the waves.

She'd journey through jungles and deserts.
She'd even find places unknown.
And, if she became an explorer,
she'd finally leave me alone.

Somewhere, Sometime

I'm going somewhere sometime,
to do something someday.
I'll go with someone somehow
to be someplace someway.

I don't know where, but nowhere
has nothing there to see.
And so I know that nowhere
is no place I should be.

To go with no one nowhere
is nothing but a bummer.
So, sometime, I'll go somewhere
with somebody some summer.

I Went to the Movies

One night I was bored, so, at 7:15,
I went to the movies and climbed in the screen.
I instantly found I was part of a scene
where aliens landed their flying machine.
They caught me and took me to meet with their queen.
Her teeth were enormous. Her face was all green.
Her head was the shape of a garbanzo bean.
She said they were going to cut out my spleen.
I never knew alien queens were so mean!
I let out a yell like a crazed wolverine,
and jumped out the window and got away clean
by taking command of a spy submarine,
and sailing away underwater, unseen.
The audience cheered as I climbed from the screen.
This film was like nothing that they'd ever seen.

I got to ride home in a sweet limousine.
My picture appeared on a film magazine
that said I was now the world's most famous teen.
I thought this was awesome, and so I was keen
to do it again. It became my routine.
And now every evening, at 7:15,
I go to the movies and climb in the screen.

Pickle with Cheddar

There's nothing I like more
than pickle with cheddar.
You really should try it.
There's nothing that's better.

The pickle is salty.
The cheddar is creamy.
The combo, together,
is utterly dreamy.

The cheddar is silky.
The pickle is crunchy.
The taste is delicious.
It's yummy and munchy.

I eat it for breakfast.
I eat it for lunch.
I eat it for dinner,
dessert, snack, and brunch.

I savor the flavor;
it cannot be beat.
But pickle with cheddar's
not *all* that I eat.

Occasionally,
since I'm just a bit fickle,
I'll try something different,
like cheddar with pickle.

The Geese Are Honking Overhead

The geese are honking overhead.
The ducks are quacking loudly.
The crows are cawing up above.
The swans are snorting proudly.

The eagles cry. The hawks reply.
The blackbirds beat their wings.
The finches twitter in the sky
as every starling sings.

The pigeons coo. The owls hoo-hoo.
The robins chirp and cheep.
The sparrows whistle warmly while
the swifts and swallows peep.

I love the sound when they're around;
so lively, wild, and free.
I simply wish that, as they passed,
they dropped no plops on me.

Our Baseball Team Is Always Last

Our baseball team is always last.
Our pitcher's "fastball" isn't fast.
Our batters never hit the ball.
Our catcher cannot catch at all.

Our runners always run too slow.
Our basemen like to watch grass grow.
Our shortstop stops a bit too short.
Our fielders don't enjoy the sport.

We've never won a single game,
and only have ourselves to blame.
Until we get some different players
We can't do much but say our prayers.

I Went to a Wishing Well

I went to a wishing well,
tossed in a penny,
and made a few wishes.
In fact, I made many.

I wished I were famous.
I wished I could fly.
I wished I were rich,
and a rock star or spy.

I wished for a robot
to do all my chores,
a dog that could talk,
and a few dinosaurs.

I wished for a dragon
and unicorn too.
Regrettably, none of
my wishes came true.

I made lots of wishes
but didn't get any.
I guess, these days,
wishes cost more than a penny.

My Grandma Bought a Rocking Chair

My grandma bought a rocking chair
and mounted it on wheels.
She rides it all around the town.
She loves the way it feels.

I've never seen her happier
than speeding down the hills
and jumping off of skateboard ramps
to demonstrate her skills.

Then grandma whoops and hollers
when her rocker catches air.
It's fun to see her soaring
in her awesome rocking chair.

She's not some kind of maniac.
She hasn't lost control.
She got this chair because, you see,
she likes to rock and roll.

The Cow on the Hill

The cow that you see
eating grass on a hill
is doing a lot more
than just standing still.

She nibbles the grass
and she sips from the stream,
to make into milk
and convert into cream.

And that's how we get
all our milk, cheese, and butter.
The grass goes in one end
and milk out the udder.

My Ice Cream Is Melting

My ice cream is melting
this hot sunny day.
I'm licking it quick but
it's dribbling away.

My ice cream is melting.
It's starting to drip
all over my fingers,
my chin, and my lip.

My ice cream is melting.
I can't make it stop.
It's hitting the ground with
a splash and a plop.

My ice cream has melted
and turned into ooze.
It *was* in a cone but
it's now on my shoes.

My Hot Dog Is Soggy

My hot dog is soggy.
My burger is wet.
My chicken is dripping.
I'm getting upset.

My corn on the cob
and my coleslaw and pie
are so full of water
I think I might cry.

My chips are like liquid
along with my fruit.
My kids are all giggling.
They think that it's cute.

I promise you this...
That's the last time that I
let them play with the hose
on the Fourth of July.

Candy Andy

Hello, my name is Andy.
I'm a fan of eating candy.
It's delicious and it's dandy,
and my favorite thing to eat.

When I want some sweets for eating,
I'll be at your door repeating
that fantastic, famous greeting…
I'll be shouting, "Trick or treat!"

I'll be dressed up like a mummy,
out in search of something yummy,
like a chocolate bar or gummi.
I'll be marching door-to-door.

And, as long as you have dishes
full of candy so delicious
you can satisfy my wishes,
I'll keep coming back for more.

You might think I'm being sneaky,
or perhaps a little cheeky,
and some people say it's freaky,
and they often ask me why…

And they tell me that it's cheating
to be on their doorstep beating
on the front door, trick-or-treating,
in the middle of July.

Mrs. Mandy's Candy Shop

At Mrs. Mandy's Candy Shop,
you cannot buy a lollipop.
You cannot purchase candy canes,
or bubble gum or Mary Janes.

They will not sell you candy bars,
or lemon drops, or sugar stars,
or licorice, or ice cream cones,
or chocolates shaped like mobile phones.

They used to carry lots of treats
but now they don't have any sweets.
And so, if you're in need of candy,
please don't visit Mrs. Mandy.

She doesn't sell it anymore.
Her store is now a hardware store,
and Mrs. Mandy is to blame
since she forgot to change the name.

Random Recipe

If you want to make a muffin,
first you need a jar of juice,
and a pickle, and a peanut,
and a marble, and a moose.

Then you add a dozen doorknobs,
and a boy with a balloon,
plus the sound of summer thunder
from a Thursday afternoon.

Then you mix them in whatever
bowl or bucket you can find.
Oh, wait. That's not the recipe.
I'm sorry. Never mind.

If You're Swallowed by an Elephant

If you're swallowed by an elephant,
you need not be afraid.
When you're sitting in his stomach,
don't be nervous or dismayed.

You might wonder how it happened.
You might ask the reasons why.
But you won't get any answers
and it doesn't help to cry.

The solution here is simple.
There's no need to scream and shout.
But, instead, just run around and 'round
until you're all pooped out.

I Went Out Exploring

I went out exploring
for treasure today.
I wasn't successful
I'm sorry to say.

Instead of some treasure
I found a few rocks.
I found a dead bug and
some stinky old socks.

I found a small string
from a party balloon,
a bubblegum wrapper,
and half of a spoon.

I found a flat can and
the cap from a pen.
I don't think that I'll go
exploring again.

Transportation Vacation

We went on vacation,
my family and I.
We got on an airplane
and flew through the sky.

We got off the airplane
and boarded a bus
that went to where taxis
were waiting for us.

We hopped in a taxi
and drove to the shore,
then rode in a boat
for an hour or more.

The boat dropped us off
and we climbed on a train
that went to the airport.
We got on a plane.

The plane took us home.
What a boring vacation!
We didn't see anything;
just transportation.

The First Day of School

Today is the day that we go back to school.
My family's excited! We all think it's cool.

We know we'll have homework and study like crazy.
We won't have a chance to relax and be lazy.

We'll wake up each morning. We'll fill up our packs
and hoist them and haul them to school on our backs.

We'll work from the morning till late every night.
We'll practice our math, and we'll read and we'll write.

For month after month we'll have so much to do.
I'm sure that this might sound unpleasant to you.

So, why are we having this grand celebration?
Today we start planning next summer's vacation.

The Birds Are Chirping Happily

The birds are chirping happily.
The lizards love their song.
The worms are winding lazily
and slithering along.

The fish are blowing bubbles
while the crickets chirp and hop.
The mice are running 'round and 'round
and never seem to stop.

The turtles slowly stretch and yawn.
The ferrets jump and slide.
The guinea pigs are burrowing.
The snakes glide side-to-side.

The bunnies bounce around their cage.
The ducklings dive and flap.
The hamsters and the hedgehogs
are relaxing with a nap.

Our teacher keeps so many pets.
It's what she likes to do,
because, before she worked at school,
she used to run the zoo.

I've Started Learning Honkish

I've started learning Honkish.
It's my favorite language now.
I'm also learning Mooish.
I can speak just like a cow.

I'm learning Chirpish, Burpish,
Beepish, and some Sneezanese,
and a dialect of Buzzish
so I sound just like the bees.

My dad taught me Snorwegian,
plus some Ancient Garglese,
and I'm fluent in a dozen other
languages like these.

I'm something of a prodigy
where language is concerned,
except for ones the language teacher
says I should have learned.

She tried to teach me Spanish,
French, and German, but I'm lazy.
And, anyway, I'd rather learn
the ones that drive her crazy.

Octopus for Lunch

The other kids
like chicken nuggets,
hot dogs, or taquitos,
or burgers, fries,
or pizza pies,
or bean and cheese burritos.

But, as for me,
I'm strange, you see,
and what I like to munch
is just a plate
of marinated
octopus for lunch.

Octopus for lunch!
Oh, octopus for lunch!
It seems I've quite
an appetite
for octopus for lunch.

While they want lots
of tater tots,
or cheesy ravioli,
or seasoned beef
on lettuce leaf,
or chips with guacamole,

I like to eat
this tasty treat
and wash it down with punch:
A steaming bowl
or casserole
of octopus for lunch.

Octopus for lunch!
Oh, octopus for lunch!
I just can't wait
to fill my plate
with octopus for lunch.

But now I find
I've changed my mind.
Indeed, I have a hunch
I'd better wait
and leave this plate
of octopus for lunch.

This plate is full
of tentacles
that waved around a bunch.
The way they sway
it seems that they
like little kids for lunch.

Octopus at lunch!
An octopus at lunch!
So run away
or else it may...
gergrabble... gobble... crunch!

My Brother Plays Dungeons & Dragons

My brother plays Dungeons & Dragons
with friends, or at home by himself.
But when he plays Dungeons & Dragons,
he isn't a wizard or elf.

He isn't a knight or a fighter.
He isn't a cleric or bard.
He isn't a rogue or a ranger,
or even a servant or guard.

He isn't a demon or dragon.
He isn't an ape or an orc.
No, when he plays Dungeons & Dragons,
he's simply, and proudly, a dork.

Mr. Right

My friends all call me Mr. Right
because I'm never wrong.
I brag about it every night.
I shout it all day long.

I always have the answers
which I'll gladly share with you.
I never need to listen.
I already know what's true.

I value your opinion when
it's just the same as mine.
As long as you agree with me
we'll get along just fine.

So, ask me and I'll tell you.
There is nothing I don't know.
I'm certain my beliefs are facts.
They're absolutely so.

And why am I so sure I have
the perfect point of view?
I heard it from somebody else
who told me it was true.

My Left Left

I woke up this morning,
a little past dawn,
completely surprised that
my left leg was gone.

And that's when I noticed,
with rising alarm,
as well as my left leg,
I'd lost my left arm.

In fact, I was missing
my body's left side.
I felt so astonished
I practically cried.

I don't know what happened
while sleeping last night.
But, don't be too worried...
I think I'm all right.

My World Is Turning Downside-Up

My world is turning downside-up.
I'm really not top-tip.
My life is feeling outside-in.
I've had a big flop-flip.

My brain feels like a mashmish
that got stepped on by Kong King.
My mind is goosey-loosey
like I'm just a dumb dong-ding.

My life's not peasy-easy.
It's not so duper-super.
It feels more like the podgehodge
from inside a scooper-pooper.

But, still, I know what life's about...
I'll do the Pokey-Hokey,
and turn myself around until
I'm feeling dokey-okey.

I'm Srot of Srcmabled Up Tdaoy

I'm srot of srcmabled up tdaoy.
I'm tolatly cnofsued.
You mgiht tihnk taht it's fnuny, but
I'm relaly not amsued.

I'm feeilng srot of sctaterbarined.
I'm trleuy in a tzizy.
I'm jsut not thniknig stragiht at all.
I'm afwluly dzaed and dzizy.

I msut be hrad to udnersatnd.
My wrods are scuh a jmuble.
My mnid feles lkie it msised a setp
and took a ltitle tmuble.

My haed is suepr wozoy and
I'm wbobly on my legs.
I geuss I sholudn't strat the day
by etaing scrmabled eggs.

Saturday's My Lazy Day

Saturday's my lazy day.
I sleep until it's noon,
then stay in bed and play a game
or watch a new cartoon.

And then I like to read a book
or maybe take a nap,
or snuggle with my kitten when
she cuddles on my lap.

I'll search around the internet.
I'll fiddle with my phone.
It's nice to have a lazy day
to goof off on my own.

There's truly nothing better.
It's what Saturdays are for.
I only wish my children would
stop banging on my door.

I'd Like to Sing in Singapore

I'd like to sing in Singapore
or run around Iran.
I'd leave my den in Denmark,
and go pack in Pakistan.

I'd fill up in the Philippines,
then take a spin through Spain
to buy a new umbrella for
the rain around Bahrain.

I'd love to rush to Russia
and perhaps pursue Peru,
but then I'd wait around Kuwait
and chill in Chile too.

I'd bang around in Bangladesh.
I'd roam around in Rome.
Then finish up in Finland
right before I headed home.

I'd like to sing in Singapore.
I've heard it's fun to do.
I know you can in Canada.
Can you in Kenya too?

I Got a New Game for My Brother

I got a new game for my brother.
My mom and my dad got upset.
They said, "You should never do something
that, later, you'll come to regret."

I nodded and told them, "I'm sorry,"
then sat back and smiled as I played.
I got a new game for my brother,
and *that* was an excellent trade.

My Parents Both Are Humans

My parents both are humans
which explains the reason why
I can't breathe underwater,
and I never learned to fly.

I can't run like a cheetah, and
I can't sting like a bee.
I can't swing through the jungle
on a vine from tree to tree.

I have no shell for shelter
like a turtle or a snail.
I can't squirt water from a trunk
or grab things with a tail.

Because my mom's a human
and my dad's a human too
I can't do all the awesome things
that other creatures do.

I have to do what humans do
instead of stuff that's cool.
My parents both are humans
so I have to go to school.

We Bought a Lot of Candy Bars

We bought a lot of candy bars.
We thought it would be neat
to have a ton for all the kids
who came to trick-or-treat.

We bought them early in the month
when they were all on sale.
We dragged the bags in from the car
and set them on the scale.

The candy weighed a hundred pounds!
I'm sure we got enough.
In fact, we may have had too much
of all that yummy stuff.

It wouldn't hurt to just eat one,
or two, or three, or four.
We bought so much that we could
even eat a dozen more.

So every day we had a few;
a minuscule amount.
How many? I can't say for sure.
I wasn't keeping count.

Our pile grew smaller every day
by ten, fifteen, or twenty.
But, still, it didn't matter.
We were certain we had plenty.

When Halloween arrived, we checked
the candy situation,
and found that we had given in
to way too much temptation.

A single bar was all we had.
We'd eaten all the rest.
So, if our lights are off tonight,
I think that's for the best.

It's Halloween, My Face Is Green

It's Halloween. My face is green.
My neck bolts both are tight.
I'm eight feet tall. My coat's too small.
I'm ready for a fight.

If you see me, you'd better flee,
or bring your clubs and torches.
They might protect, but don't expect
to chase me off your porches.

Your village square? I'll lumber there.
I'll shamble to your door.
I'll grunt and groan and wail and moan.
I'll shout and shriek and roar.

I'll have you scared, so be prepared,
and keep your pitchforks handy.
I'm Frankenstein. I've come to dine.
Please give me all your candy.

A Vampire Bit My Neck Last Night

A vampire bit my neck last night
and, though it sounds insane,
some zombies chased me down the street
and tried to eat my brain.

A mummy shambled after me.
Godzilla stomped my face.
I nearly got abducted by
an alien from space.

When Frankenstein attacked me
I escaped, but then almost
got tackled by a skeleton,
a werewolf, and a ghost.

A slimy blob engulfed me.
Then I woke up with a scream.
I've never been so overjoyed
to wake up from a dream.

Last night I learned a lesson:
If you want to keep your head,
don't watch a scary movie
right before you go to bed.

My Brother Might Be Bigfoot

My brother might be bigfoot.
I've seen a bunch of clues.
He's very hairy, super tall,
and wears enormous shoes.

Whenever I say hi to him
my brother starts to growl.
He walks like a gorilla
and his fetid stench is foul.

He never takes a shower so
he's slovenly and sweaty.
He claims to have a girlfriend too;
he says her name is Yeti.

He's not a myth. From what I've seen
I think we can assume
that bigfoot lives among us...
He's in my brother's room.

I'd Like to Meet an Alien

I'd like to meet an alien.
Yeah, wouldn't that be neat?
I'm sure there's not another
creature I would rather meet.

I wouldn't care if he was big,
or medium, or tiny,
or if his skin was rough and tough,
or super smooth and shiny.

I'd like him if his head were bald
or covered up with hair.
I'd like him if his face were round,
triangular, or square.

He could be colored black and white,
or yellow, red, and green.
He might be awfully dirty
or meticulously clean.

I'd like him if he whispered
and I'd like him if he yelled.
I'd like him if he used perfume
or positively smelled.

It wouldn't matter much to me
if he was soft or scaly,
or if he danced the rhumba,
or he played the ukulele.

He could look like a lizard,
or be furry and mammalian.
I'd simply like to scare my mom
by bringing home an alien.

The Dog Ate Our Dinner

The table was set for Thanksgiving this year.
Our aunts and our uncles and cousins were here.
Our parents had put out our holiday feast,
and that's when our doggy turned into a beast.

He jumped on the table and wolfed down the hams.
He polished off all the potatoes and yams.
He gobbled the turkey, the gravy, and greens,
then swallowed the stuffing and all the green beans.

He crammed down the cranberry sauce and the rolls,
and licked every morsel of food from the bowls.
And, when we at last got ahold of our dog,
his lips were still dripping with pie and eggnog.

It's sort of a shame, but it's totally clear
we're going to have to be careful next year
if we want some pie or potatoes or meat,
since this year we only have dog food to eat.

I Dreamed It Was December

I dreamed it was December
and the trees were draped in snow,
that Christmas would be coming;
just a few more weeks to go.

I dreamed we'd have a holiday,
a festive winter break.
We'd give each other presents
and we'd feast on pie and cake.

I dreamed we'd decorate the house
to celebrate the Yule.
And, best of all, we'd get
a little time away from school.

I dreamed I'd make a snowman
and go sliding on my sled.
But then I heard my mother saying,
"Wake up sleepyhead."

I dreamed it was December
and would soon be New Year's Day.
It stinks to have that dream
and then find out it's only May.

Our Holiday Shopping

Our parents went holiday shopping online.
They ordered the presents and thought it was fine.
But, then, they forgot to turn off the computer,
and that's when the baby, who couldn't be cuter,
decided to play with the keyboard awhile.
She climbed up and pushed a few keys with a smile.

She bought a new blanket, a book, and a binkie,
a bottle, some blocks, and a sled, and a Slinky.
She ordered a dozen new puzzles and balls,
plus hundreds of teddy bears, diapers, and dolls.
And when she was done clicking keys for the day,
she giggled and got down and waddled away.

The cat came along and walked over the keys
and ordered some cat toys and treatments for fleas.
Our puppy jumped up and bought toys he could chew,
plus sweaters, and leashes, and tennis balls too.
And, lastly, our hamster sat down on the mouse,
and clicked to have everything shipped to our house.

The presents arrived just a day or two later.
I don't think I've ever seen anything greater!
The drivers arrived and, before they were gone,
left thousands of packages out on our lawn.
It's all so exciting, and will be until
our parents receive their next credit card bill.

Hip-Hop Christmas

The North Pole has a DJ.
His name is M.C. Kringle.
He loves to spin a record or
to sing a Christmas jingle.

He'll b-boy on the dance floor
to disco, rap, and rock.
He'll beatbox on the microphone,
then stop and pop and lock.

He likes to do the Robot.
He loves to rap a rhyme.
The elves and reindeer always watch
and stomp their feet in time.

They'll wiggle to the rhythm.
You'll sometimes see them clapping.
You see, his helpers make the gifts
but Santa does the rapping.

On New Year's Day

On New Year's Day a year ago,
I kicked a rock and broke my toe.
Then February came around;
I slipped on ice and smacked the ground.

In March I tripped and skinned my knee.
In April, met an angry bee.
In May a baseball hit my hip.
In June I bit my lower lip.

I banged my elbow in July.
When August came, I poked my eye.
September, I fell out of bed.
October's when I hurt my head.

November, had a nasty fall.
December, crashed into a wall.
So, you can truly not believe
how glad I am it's New Year's Eve.

Though, this year, I was so annoyed,
at least I know what to avoid
beginning January first.
Goodbye, last year. You were the worst.

Index

Astrocow 14

Birds Are Chirping Happily, The 84

Book of Glue, The 38

Candy Andy 74

Computer Cat 10

Cow on the Hill, The 70

Crash! Bang! Boom! 18

Dog Ate Our Dinner, The 114

Elaine the Complainer 24

Elephant Repairman, The 8

First Day of School, The 83

Geese Are Honking Overhead, The 64

Hip-Hop Christmas 120

How to Eat a Chocolate Bunny 56

I Dreamed It Was December 116

I Got a New Game for My Brother 102

I Hypnotized the Teacher 22

I Like It When It's Quiet 33

I Love to Read a Mystery 36

I Think I'd Like to Get a Pet......................26

I Tried to Find a Dinosaur........................21

I Went Out Exploring 80

I Went to a Wishing Well 66

I Went to the Movies................................60

I'd Like to Meet an Alien........................112

I'd Like to Sing in Singapore..................100

I'm Srot of Srcmabled Up Tdaoy 98

I'm Wearing My Parrot.............................41

I've Started Learning Honkish 86

If You're Swallowed by an Elephant.........79

It's Halloween, My Face Is Green...........106

Life of a Pirate Ain't Easy, The.................52

Mr. Right..92

Mr. Whisper 34

Mrs. Mandy's Candy Shop 76

My Brother Might Be Bigfoot 110

My Brother Plays Dungeons & Dragons ..91

My Brother Was Brought by a Bunny 54

My Grandma Bought a Rocking Chair.....68

My Hot Dog Is Soggy 72

My Ice Cream Is Melting..........................71

My Kitten Had an Accident 44

My Koala's Not a Doctor..........................42

My Left Left...94

My Parents Both Are Humans............... 103

My Sister Should Be an Explorer 58

My Sloth Is Supersonic 28

My World Is Turning Downside-Up 96

Noisy Boys from Boise, The.....................16

Octopus for Lunch 88

On New Year's Day................................ 122

Our Baseball Team Is Always Last 65

Our Classroom Is Covered in Sparkles....20

Our Holiday Shopping........................... 118

Our Magic Toilet 12

Overslept 46

Pickle with Cheddar 62

Please Don't Prank Your Parents 50

Random Recipe 78

Rumble in My Bedroom, A 32

Saturday's My Lazy Day 99

Somewhere, Sometime 59

Tiny Todd the Turtle 30

Today I Have a Toothache 39

Toucan Can-Can 40

Transportation Vacation 82

Vampire Bit My Neck Last Night, A 108

We Bought a Lot of Candy Bars 104

Weather Is Perfect for Running, The 45

Zoom Gloom 48

ABOUT THE AUTHOR

Children's Poet Laureate (2013-2015) Kenn Nesbitt is the author of many books for children, including *The Armpit of Doom, More Bears!, The Tighty-Whitey Spider,* and *One Minute Till Bedtime.* He is also the creator of the world's most popular children's poetry website, www.poetry4kids.com.

More Books by Kenn Nesbitt

One Minute till Bedtime – It's time for tuck-in, and your little one wants just one more moment with you–so fill it with something that will feed the imagination and send them off to sleep in a snap! Little Brown Books for Young Readers. ISBN: 978-0316341219.

Bigfoot Is Missing – Children's Poets Laureate J. Patrick Lewis and Kenn Nesbitt team up to offer a smart, stealthy tour of the creatures of shadowy myth and fearsome legend. Bigfoot, the Mongolian Death Worm, and the Loch Ness Monster number among the many creatures lurking within these pages. Chronicle Books. ISBN: 978-1452118956.

Believe it or Not, My Brother Has a Monster – From one scary monster to ten disgusting slugs and everything in between, this spooky story is full of creepy crawlies...and one nervous little brother! Scholastic. ISBN: 978-0545650595.

My Dog Likes to Disco – Seventy hilarious poems about disco-dancing dogs, invisible kids, misbehaving phones, preposterous people, and much, much more. ISBN: 979-8714869594.

My Cat Knows Karate – Another seventy poems about goofy gadgets, kooky characters, funny families, insane situations, and much, much more. ISBN: 978-1720779346.

The Biggest Burp Ever – Seventy more poems about wacky animals, comical characters, funny families, silly situations, and much, much more. ISBN: 978-1500802011.

The Armpit of Doom – Seventy new poems about crazy characters, funny families, peculiar pets, comical creatures, and much, much more. ISBN: 978-1477590287.

The Ultimate Top Secret Guide to Taking Over the World
Fed up with people telling you what to do? Read this book and in no time, you will be laughing maniacally as the world cowers before you. Sourcebooks Jabberwocky. ISBN: 978-1402238345.

MORE BEARS! – Kenn Nesbitt's picture book debut will have you laughing while shouting "More Bears!" along with the story's disruptive audience. Sourcebooks Jabberwocky. ISBN: 978-1402238352.

The Tighty-Whitey Spider: And More Wacky Animals Poems I Totally Made Up – With poems like and "I Bought Our Cat a Jetpack" and "My Dog Plays Invisible Frisbee," this collection shines with rhymes that are full of jokes, thrills, and surprises. Sourcebooks Jabberwocky. ISBN: 978-1402238338.

My Hippo Has the Hiccups: And Other Poems I Totally Made Up – *My Hippo Has the Hiccups* contains over a hundred hilarious poems. The dynamic CD brings the poems to life with Kenn reading his own poetry, cracking jokes, and telling stories. Sourcebooks Jabberwocky. ISBN: 978-1402218095.

Revenge of the Lunch Ladies: The Hilarious Book of School Poetry – From principals skipping school to lunch ladies getting back at kids who complain about cafeteria food, school has never been so funny. Meadowbrook Press. ISBN: 978-1416943648.

When the Teacher Isn't Looking: And Other Funny School Poems
When the Teacher Isn't Looking may be the funniest collection of poems about school ever written. This collection of poems by Kenn Nesbitt is sure to have you in stitches from start to finish. Meadowbrook Press. ISBN: 978-0684031286.

The Aliens Have Landed at Our School! – No matter what planet you live on, this book is packed with far-out, funny, clever poems guaranteed to give you a galactic case of the giggles. Meadowbrook Press. ISBN: 978-0689048647.

Printed in Great Britain
by Amazon